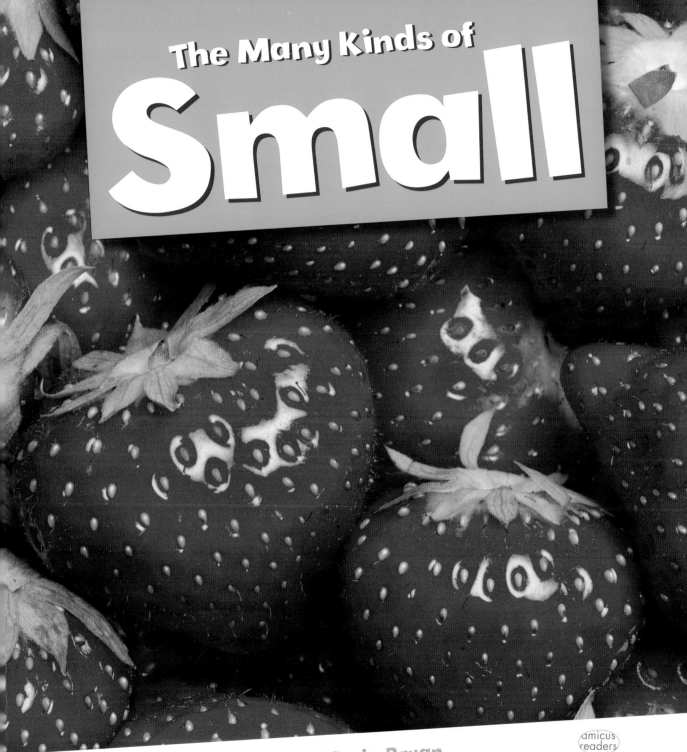

The Many Kinds of
Small

by Dale-Marie Bryan

amicus
readers

Ideas for Parents and Teachers

Amicus Readers let children practice reading informational texts at the earliest reading levels. Familiar words and concepts with close photo-text matches support early readers.

Before Reading

- Discuss the cover photo with the child. What does it tell him?
- Ask the child to predict what she will learn in the book.

Read the Book

- "Walk" through the book and look at the photos. Let the child ask questions.
- Read the book to the child, or have the child read independently.

After Reading

- Use the picture glossary at the end of the book to review the text.
- Prompt the child to make connections. Ask: What are other words for small?

Amicus Readers are published by Amicus
P.O. Box 1329, Mankato, MN 56002
www.amicuspublishing.us

Library of Congress
Cataloging-in-Publication Data
Bryan, Dale-Marie, 1953-
  The many kinds of small / Dale-Marie Bryan.
    pages cm. -- (So many synonyms)
  ISBN 978-1-60753-507-2 (hardcover) -- ISBN 978-1-60753-541-6 (eBook)
  1. English language--Synonyms and antonyms--Juvenile literature. I. Title.
  PE1591.B765 2013
  428.1--dc23
                            2013006845

Photo Credits: Richard Semik/Shutterstock Images, cover; Denis Larkin/Shutterstock Images, 1, 12, 13, 16 (middle right); Alexandra Lande/Shutterstock Images, 3; Shutterstock Images, 4, 9, 16 (top left), 16 (bottom left), 16 (bottom right); Valentyn Volkov/Shutterstock Images, 7, 16 (middle left); Sergiy Kuzmin/Shutterstock Images, 10, 11, 16 (top right); Michael Jung/Shutterstock Images, 15

Produced for Amicus by The Peterson Publishing Company and Red Line Editorial.

Editor Jenna Gleisner
Designer Becky Daum
Printed in the United States of America
Mankato, MN
July, 2013
PA 1938
10 9 8 7 6 5 4 3 2 1

Look around your kitchen.
What do you see that is small?
Are there other words that
mean small? Words with similar
meanings are synonyms.

4

Baby means small.

Baby carrots are much smaller than the carrots that grow in the garden. They are cut before they go to the store.

Little means small.

Grapes are little. They grow on vines. Many little grapes together make a bunch.

Miniature means small.

Miniature marshmallows are smaller than regular marshmallows. Many fit in a mug of hot cocoa.

Tiny means small.

Peas are tiny. They grow inside a pod. Many tiny peas can fit inside a pod.

Itsy-bitsy means small.

Strawberries are one of the only fruits with seeds on the outside. Itsy-bitsy strawberry seeds are so small we can eat them.

13

Microscopic means small.

Germs are microscopic.
They are too small to see.
We use microscopes to see and
learn about germs.

Synonyms for Small

baby
small in size

tiny
very small

little
small

itsy-bitsy
very tiny

miniature
smaller than usual

microscopic
too small to see
without a microscope